SCHIRMER'S LIBRARY OF MUSICAL CLASSICS

Vol. 383

CARL CZERNY

Op. 365

School of the Virtuoso

Studies in Bravura and Style

For the Piano

Edited and Fingered by

GIUSEPPE BUONAMICI

G. SCHIRMER, Inc.

DISTRIBUTED BY

HAL•LEONARD®
CORPORATION

7777 W. BLUEMOUND RD. P.O. BOX 13819 MILWAUKEE, WI 53213

Printed in the U. S. A.

VORWORT.

In allen Künsten ist die vollendete Beherrschung des Stoffes die erste Erforderniss der Meisterschaft, und wer Alles dessen vollkommen mächtig ist, was der Mindergeübte Schwierigkeiten nennt, der ist ein *Virtuose* (Meister) in seinem Fache. Das Studium der Schwierigkeiten auf dem *Fortepiano* ist weder so abschreckend und mühsam, wie Viele glauben, noch so überflüssig und entbehrlich, wie manche Andere behaupten;—denn nur die vollkommenste Beherrschung der mechanischen Kunst macht es möglich, die Schönheit des Vortrags und Gefuhls, welche dem einfacheren Gesange zukommt, auch auf diejenigen Stellen anzuwenden, welche dem Misskennenden oder Ungeübten nur eine Anhäufung von Unbequemlichkeiten zu sein scheinen, welche aber unter den Fingern des wahren Künstlers ebenso den Schönheitssinn befriedigen können, wie jede einfachere Melodie, und überdiess jeder Kunstleistung weit mehr Glanz und Leben verleihen. Die Vervollkommnung des *Fortepiano*, und das Bedürfniss des fortschreitenden Zeitgeschmacks macht alles dieses möglich, nothwendig, und sogar leicht. Um zu diesem bedeutenden Ziel in möglichst kurzer Zeit zu gelangen, ist bei den nachfolgenden Übungen die Zahl der ununterbrochenen Wiederholungen vorgeschrieben und festgesetzt worden, in der bewahrten Uberzeugung, dass der Studirende hiedurch schon nach einigen Monaten zu einem Grade von Fertigkeit gelangt, den er sonst auf gewöhnlichem Wege kaum in eben so vielen Jahren erreichen würde:—ein Gewinnst, der dieser Mühe und Hingebung wohl werth ist. Übrigens bleibt es natürlicherweise doch auch der Überlegung und Ausdauer des Spielers uberlassen, in wiefern er die Zahl dieser Wiederholungen abkürzen, oder allenfalls manchmal noch vermehren will. Der Verfasser ist der Meinung, dass man sich täglich ungefähr eine Stunde mit diesen Übungen beschiftigen soll. Dass übrigens Jeder, welcher dieses Werk vornimmt, bereits eine gute Schule, und Fertigkeit im Lesen haben muss, bedarf wohl keiner Erinnerung.

CARL CZERNY.

PREFACE.

In every art, a perfect control of its technics is a prime requisite of mastership, and one who has complete command of what are termed difficulties by the less skilled, is a *virtuoso* (master) in his profession. The study of the difficulties in pianoforte-playing is neither so discouraging and wearisome as many suppose, nor so superfluous and needless as many others assert ; for only the completest control of mechanical art renders it possible to employ the beauties in style and expression, which are natural to the simpler *cantilene*, in such passages also as appear, to the unobservant or unskilful, to be merely an accumulation of difficulties, but which, under the hands of a true artist, appeal to the sense of the beautiful as successfully as any simple melody, besides lending far greater brilliancy and animation to any artistic rendering. The perfection of the pianoforte, and the demands of the progressive taste of our time, make all this possible, necessary, and even easy. In order to attain to this high goal as quickly as may be, a fixed number of uninterrupted repetitions is directed for each exercise, in the conviction, approved by experience, that by this means the student can attain in a few months to a degree of proficiency which he could hardly have reached, according to the usual methods, in as many years :—a gain well worth the pains and application demanded. Of course, it must be left to the judgment and endurance of each player to decide in what cases the number of these repetitions may be diminished, or even increased. The author is of the opinion, that about one hour daily should be devoted to these exercises. Finally, it is hardly necessary to add, that every student taking up this work should possess a good technique, and read easily at sight.

CARL CZERNY

School of the Virtuoso.

Play each repeat 20 times.

C. CZERNY. Op. 365, Book I.

Printed in the U. S. A.

(1)

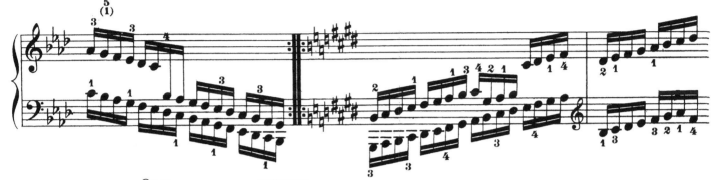

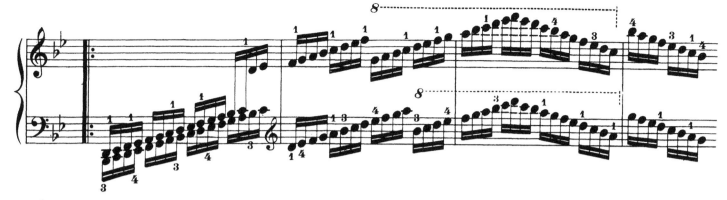

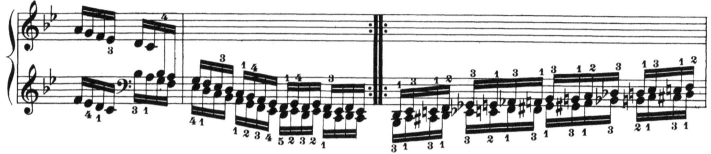

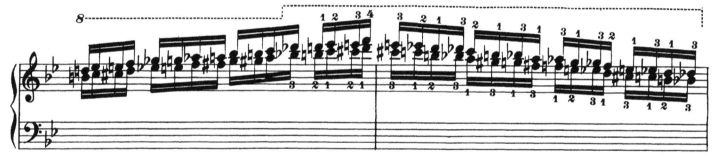

Coda.

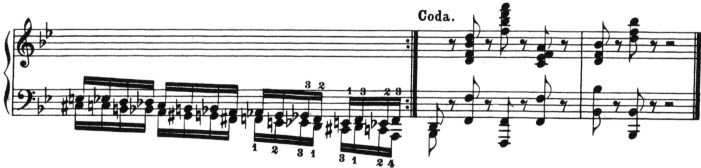

Play each repeat 16 times.

Molto Allegro. ($\textstyle\frac{}{}$ = 66.)

2.

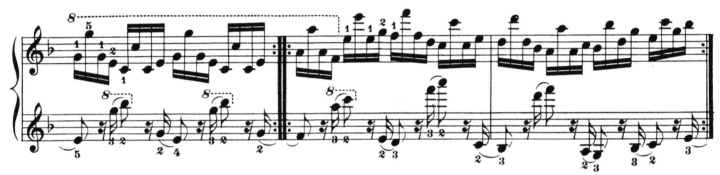

8

Play each repeat 16 times.

Molto Allegro. ($\bullet$ = 76.)

3.

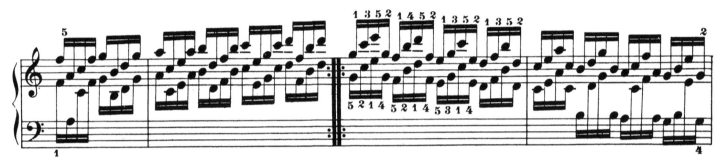

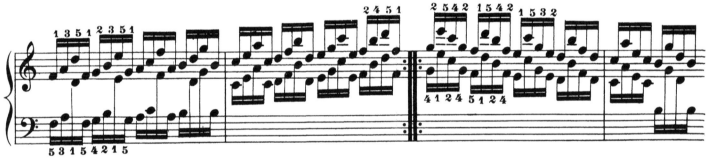

12726

Play each repeat 16 times.

Molto Allegro. ($\quad$ = 88.)

4. p^1 *velocissimo*

cresc.

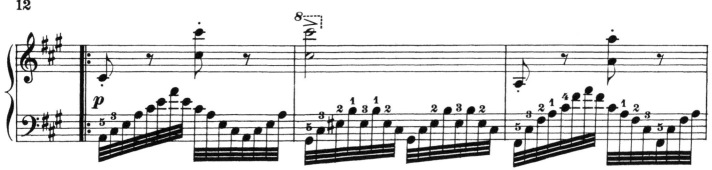

14

calando

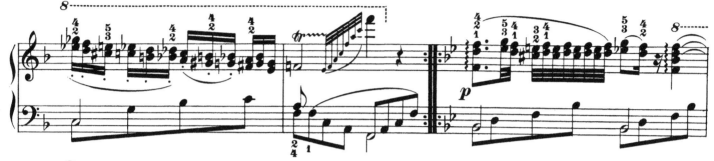

cresc.

dimin.

pp

tr

dimin.

smorz.

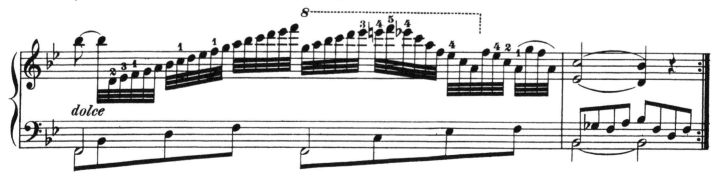

dolce

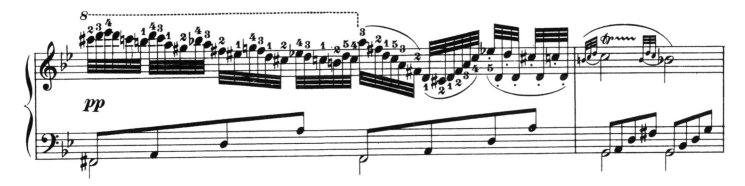

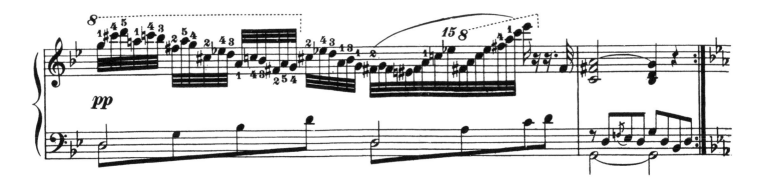

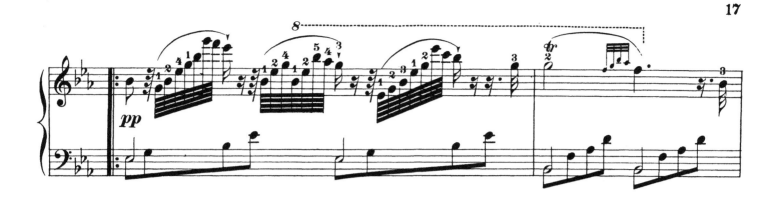

Play each repeat 16 times.

Molto Allegro velocissimo. (♩ = 112.)

6.

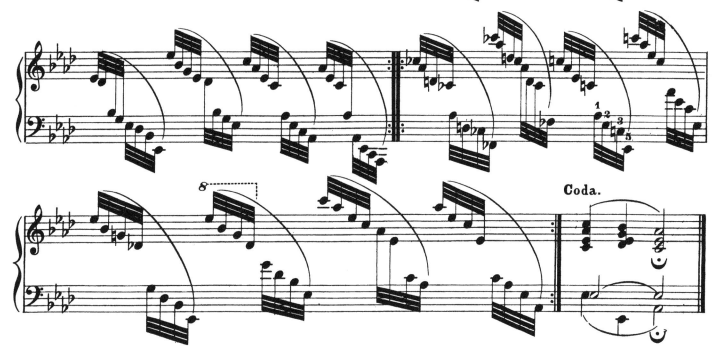

Coda.

20

Moderato. (♪ = 138.)
legato e ben marcato.

7.

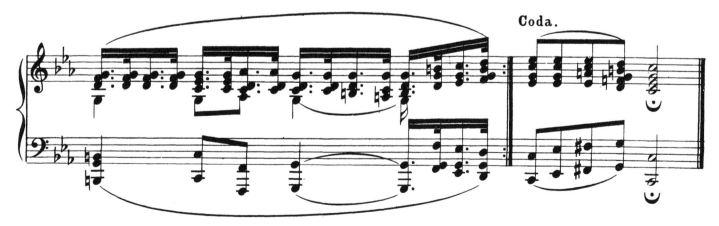

Play each repeat 20 times.

8.

12726

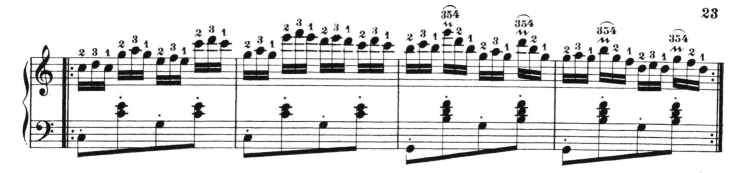

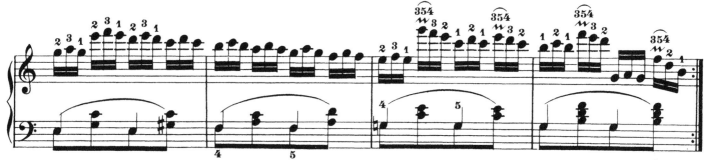

Play each repeat 12 times.

Molto Allegro. ($\mathbf{\stackrel{\flat}{=}}$ = 69.)

9.

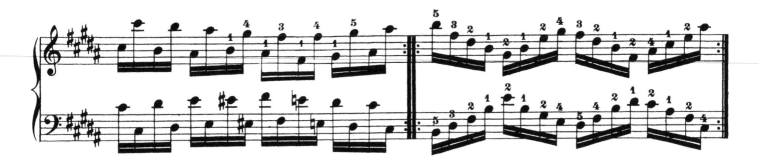

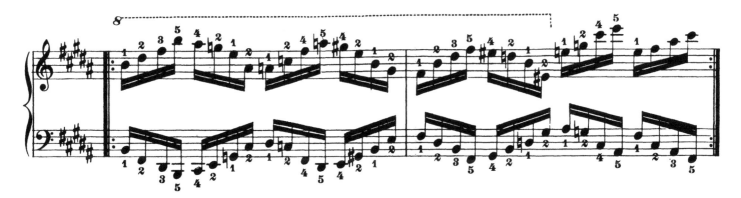

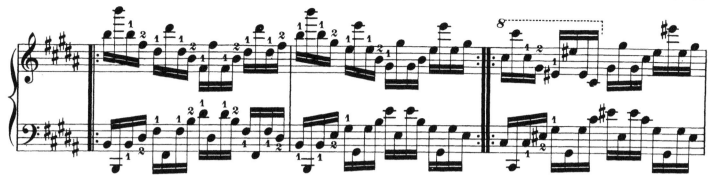

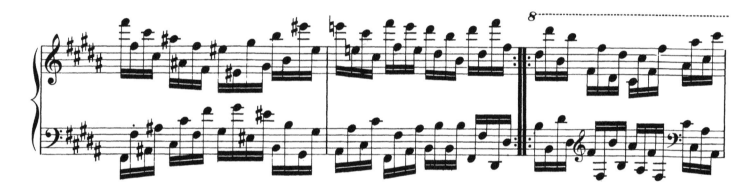

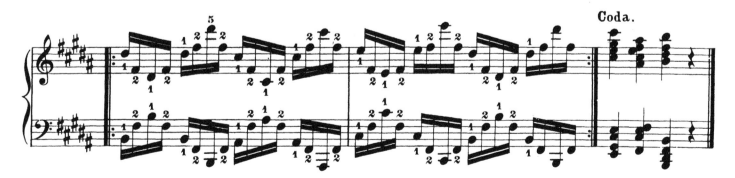

Play each repeat 8 times.

10.

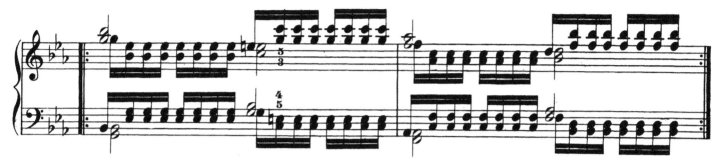

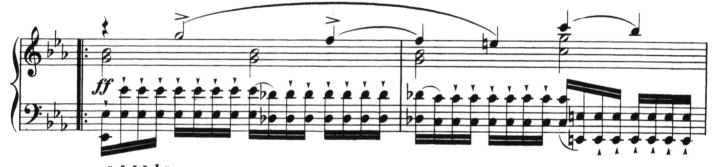

Play each repeat 20 times.

11.

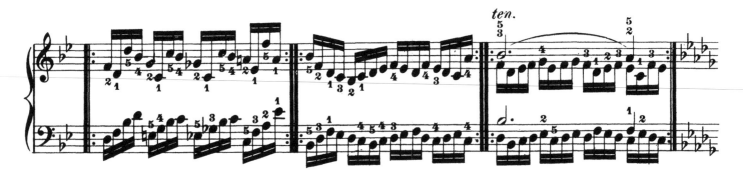

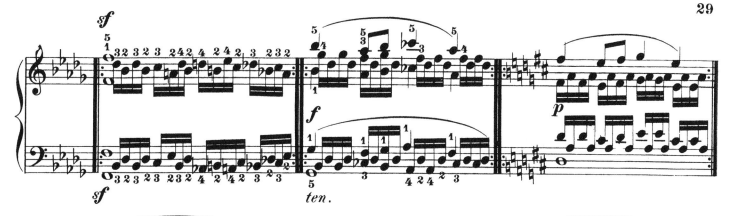

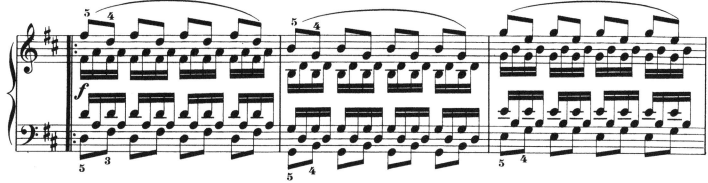

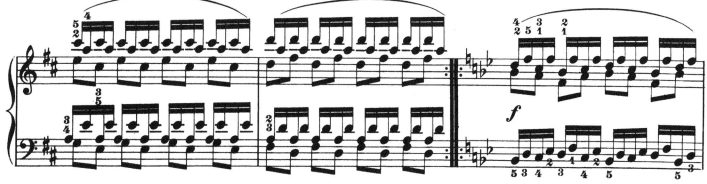

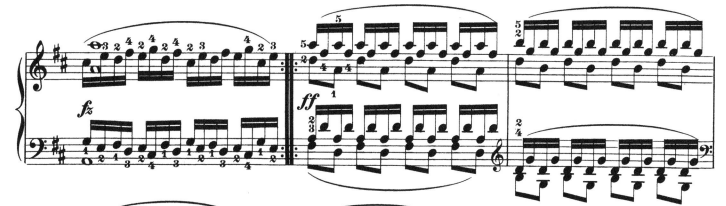

Play each repeat 16 times.

Allegro vivo. (♩ = 76.)

12.

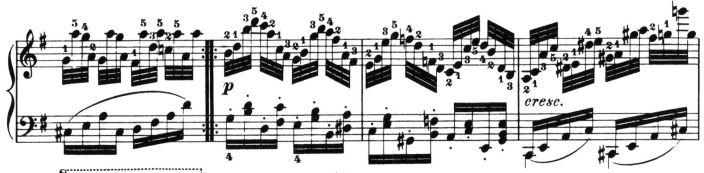

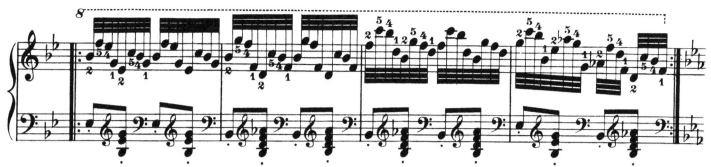

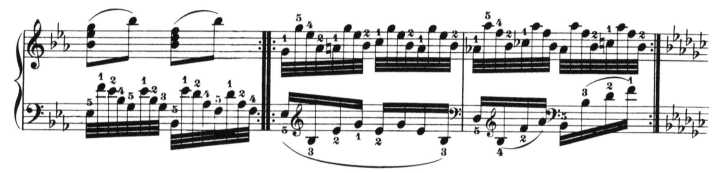

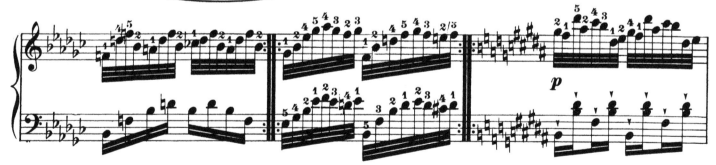

School of the Virtuoso.

Play each repeat 20 times.

C. CZERNY. Op. 365, Book II.

Molto Allegro. (♩ = 80.)

13.

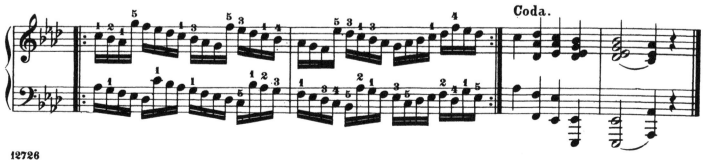

Play each repeat 20 times.

Allegro. ($\bullet$ = 112.)

14.

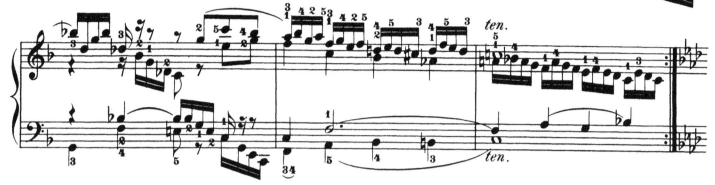

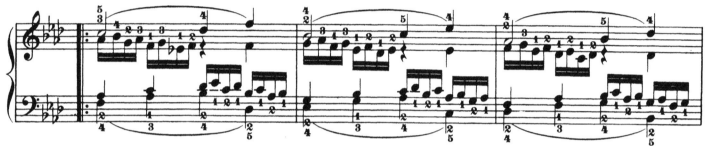

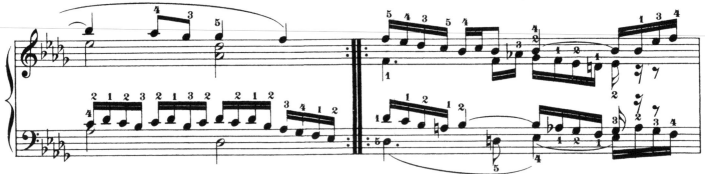

Play each repeat 20 times.

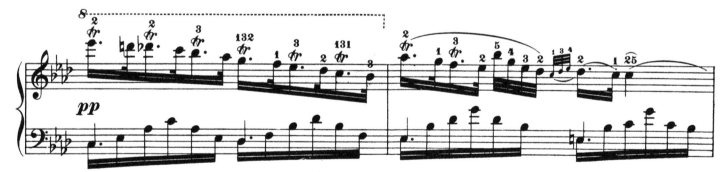

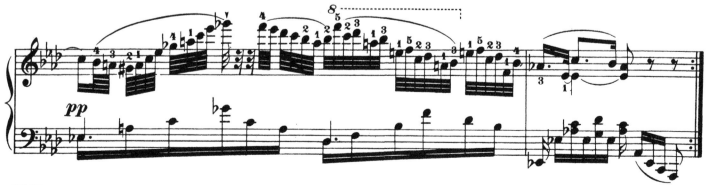

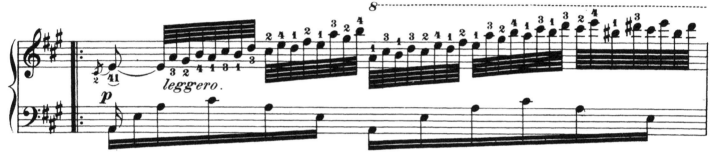

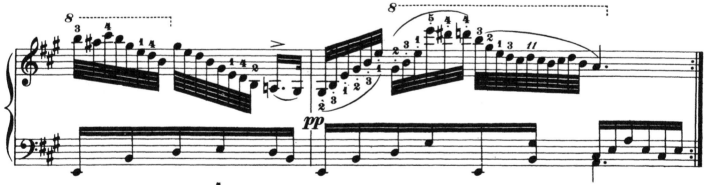

Play each repeat 8 times.

16.

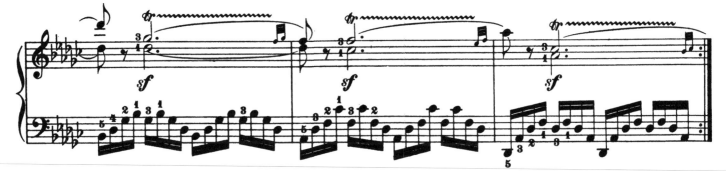

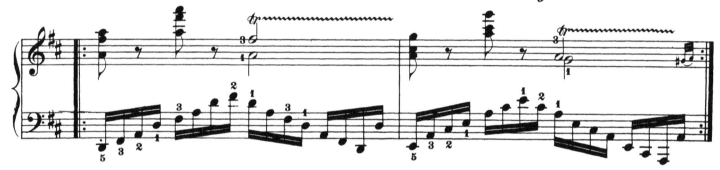

44

Allegro molto. ($\downarrow$ = 76.)

17.

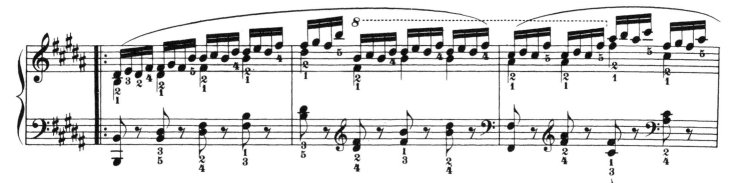

12726

Play each repeat 8 times.

Moderato quasi Andante. (♩=138.)

18.

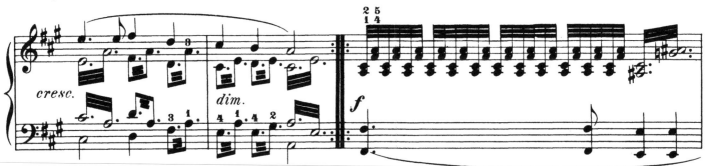

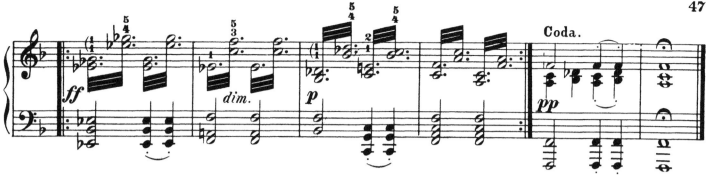

Coda.

Play each repeat 20 times.

19.

Allegro. ($\quad$ = 132.)

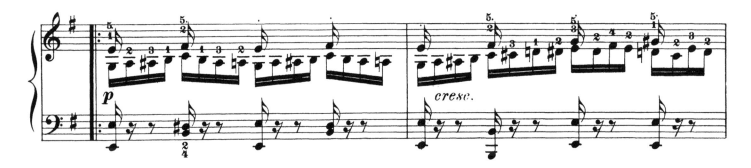

Play each repeat 16 times.

Allegro vivace. ($\bullet$ = 84)

20.

Play each repeat 16 times.

Allegro. (♩ = 116)

21.

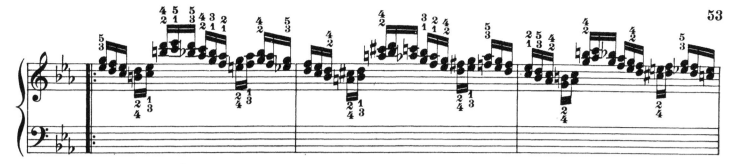

Coda.

12726

Play each repeat **20** times.

Allegro vivo. ($\bullet$ = 120)

22.

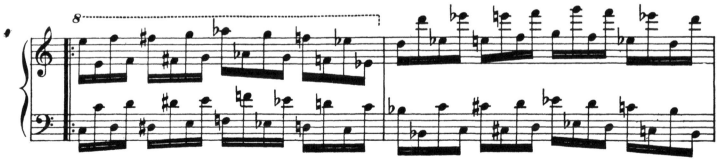

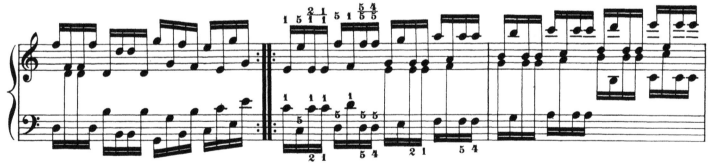

12726

Play each repeat 12 times.

Allegro. (♩ = 120)

23.

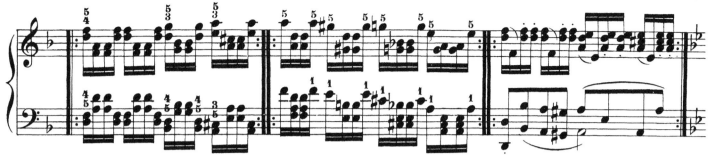

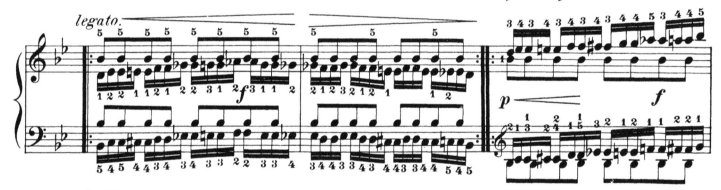

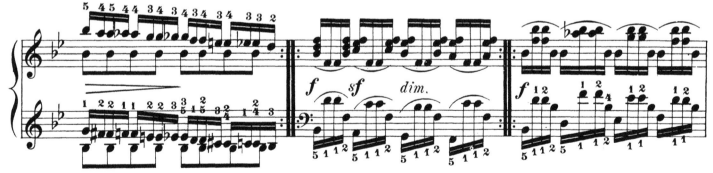

Play each repeat 20 times.

Allegro molto. ($\quad$ = 120)

24.

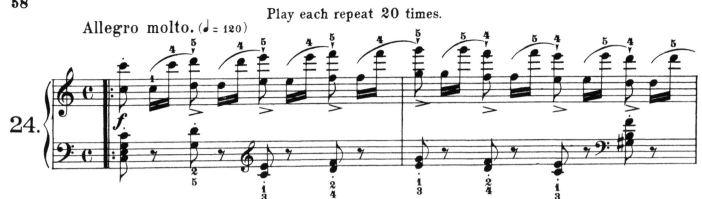

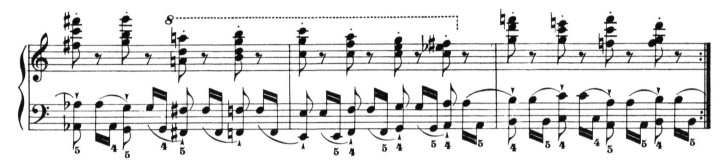

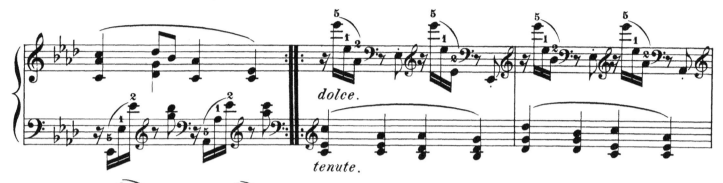

Play each repeat **20** times.

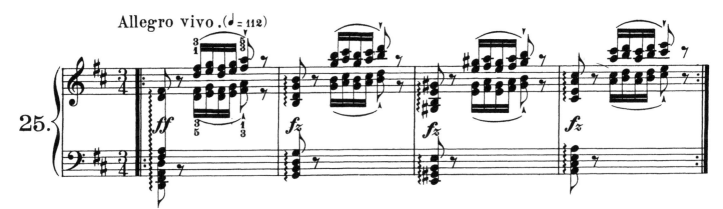

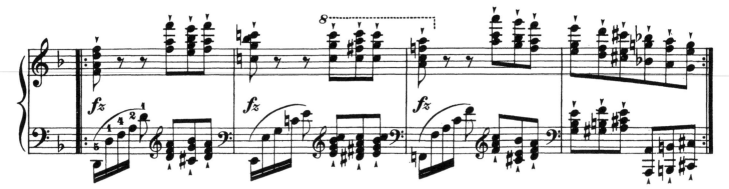

12726

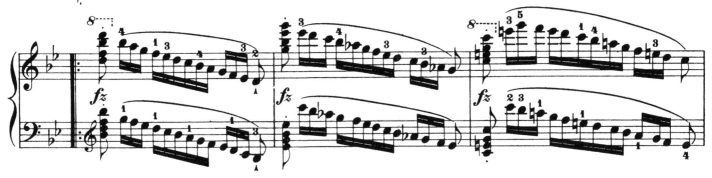

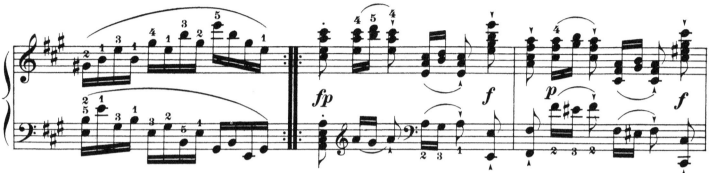

Coda.

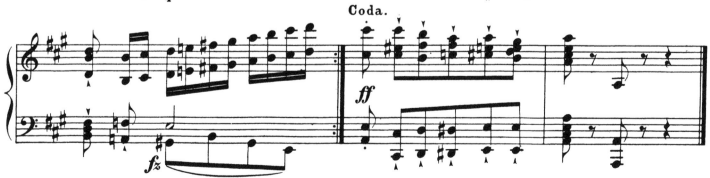

Play each repeat 12 times.

12726

Play each repeat 16 times.

Allegro vivo. ($\bullet$ = 69.)

27.

School of the Virtuoso.

Play each repeat 12 times.

C. CZERNY. Op. 365, Book III.

Allegro molto. ($\quad$ = 126.)

28.

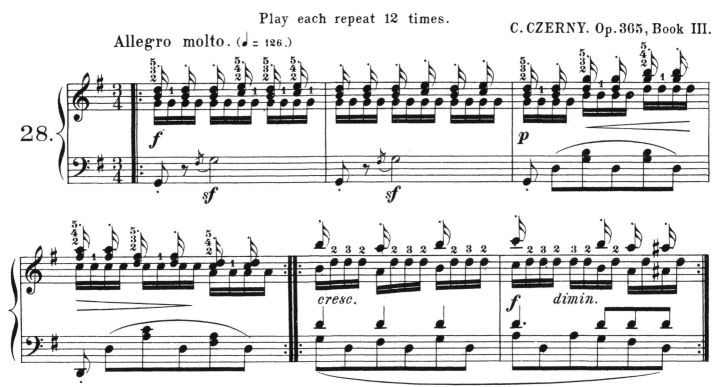

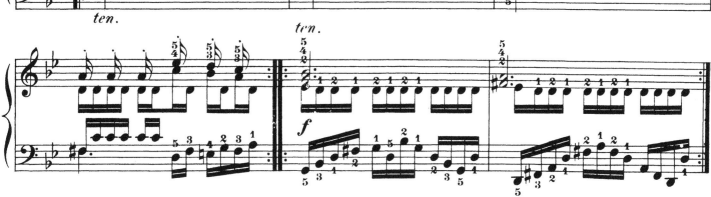

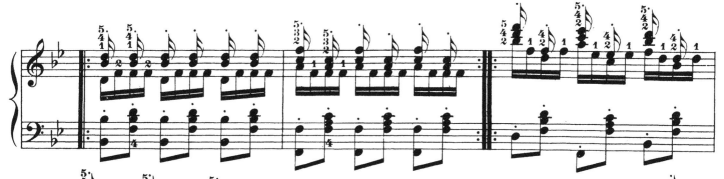

Coda.

Allegro. ($\quad = 92.$) Play each repeat 12 times.

29.

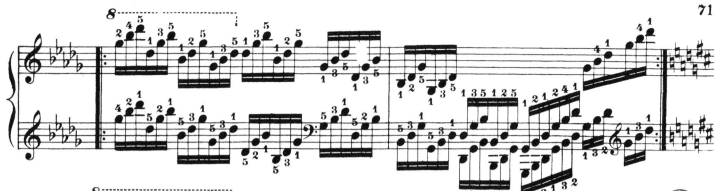

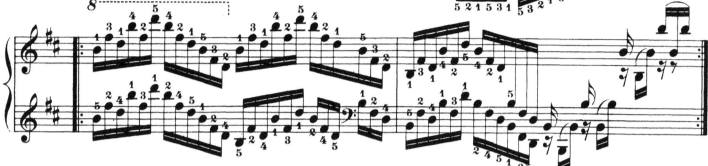

12726

Play each repeat 12 times.

Allegro molto. (♩ = 69.)

30.

Coda.

dim. e rall.   **pp**

12726

Play each repeat 8 times.

Allegro comodo. (♩ = 116.)

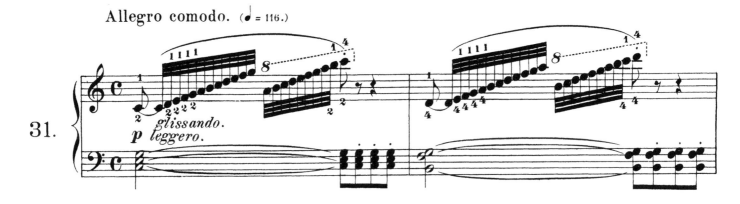

31.

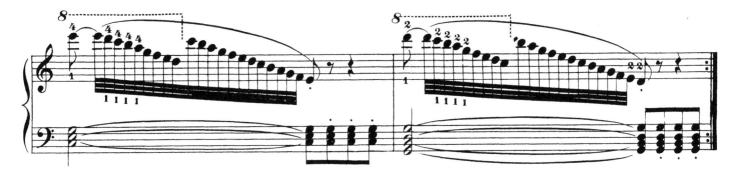

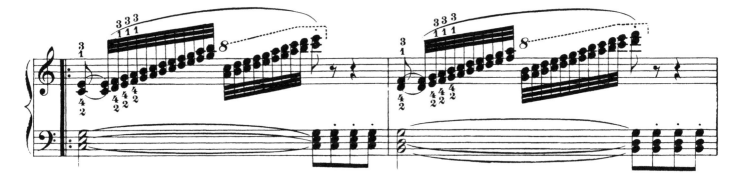

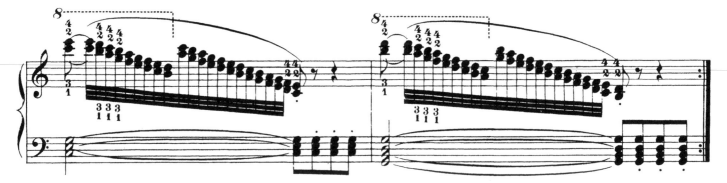

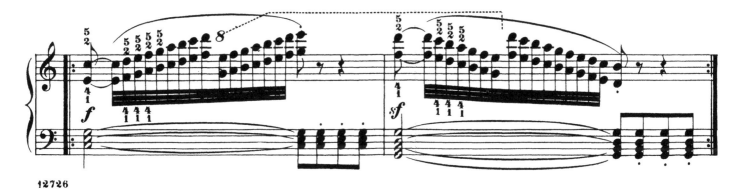

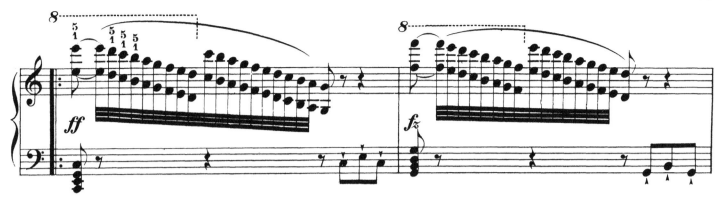

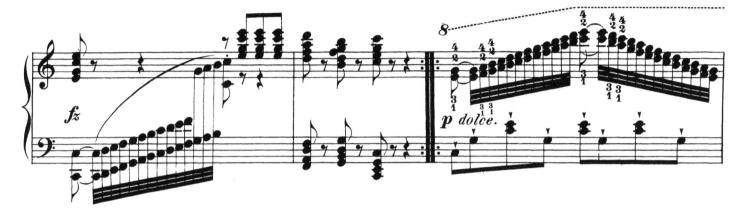

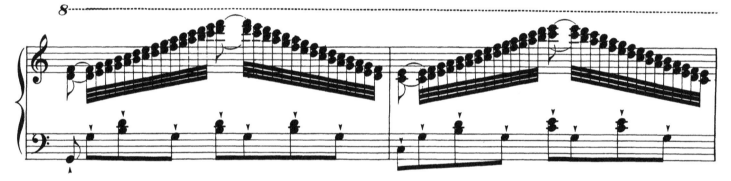

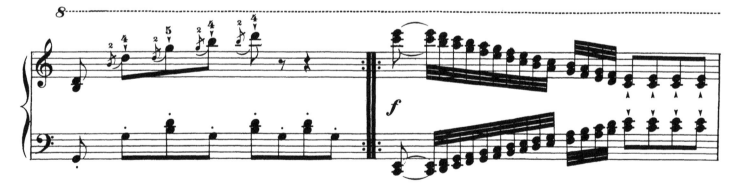

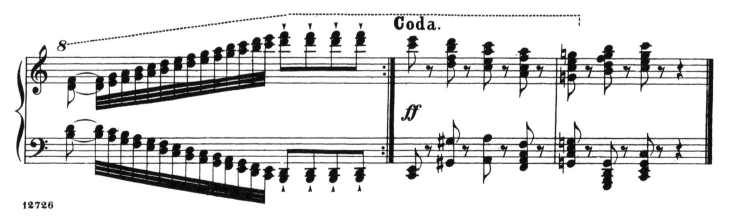

Play each repeat 12 times.

Allegro vivace. ($\dot{}$ = 144.)

32.

sempre **pp** e legg.

12726

Coda.

12726

Play each repeat 20 times.

Play each repeat **12** times.

Allegro. ($\downarrow$ = 108.)

34.

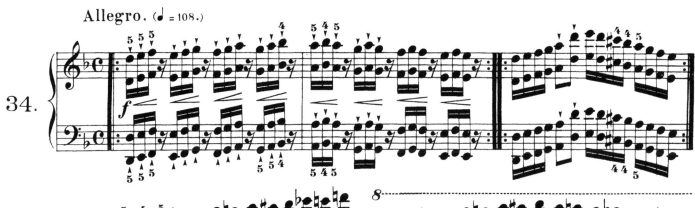

sempre f

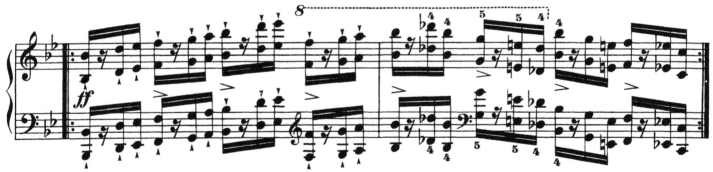

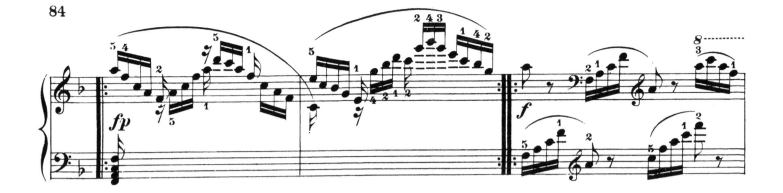

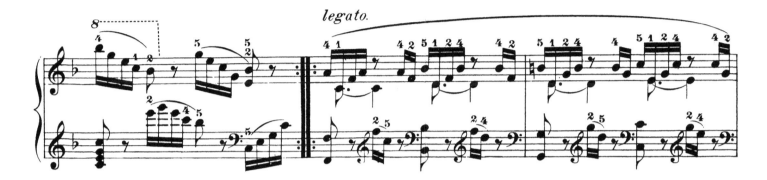

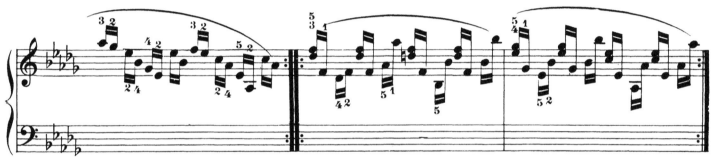

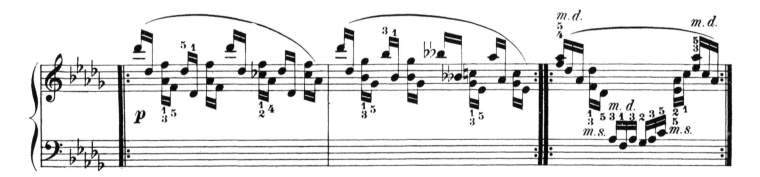

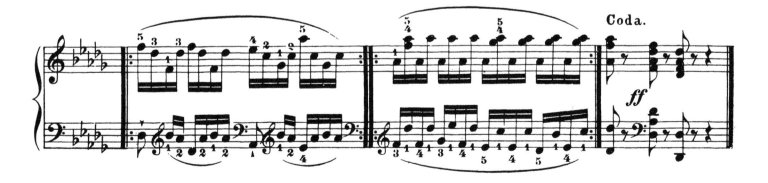

Play each repeat 30 times.

Allegro moderato. ($\bullet$ = 92)

36.

Coda.

Play each repeat 16 times.

Play each repeat 12 times.

Allegro moderato e maestoso. (♩ = 100)

Play each repeat 24 times.

Allegro moderato. (♩ = 88)

39.

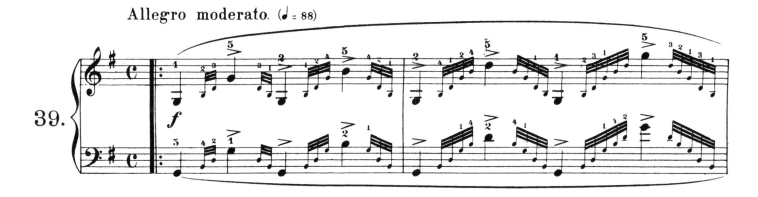

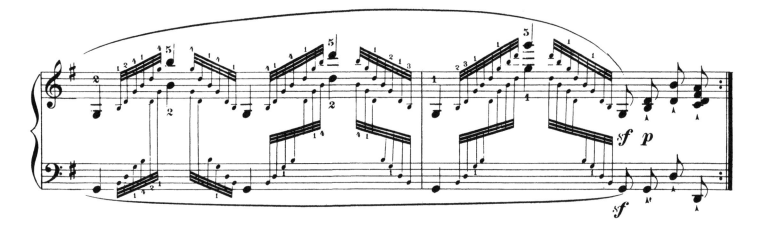

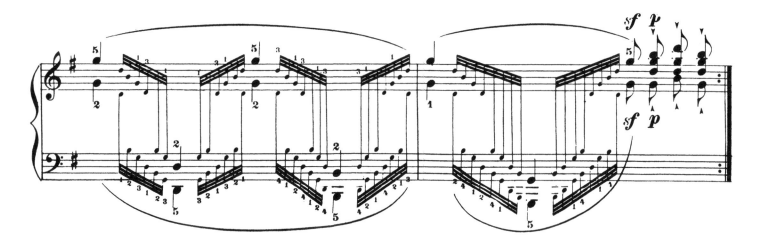

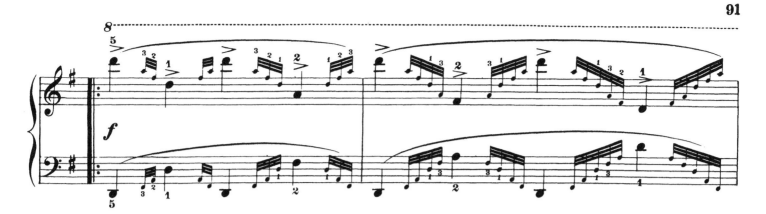

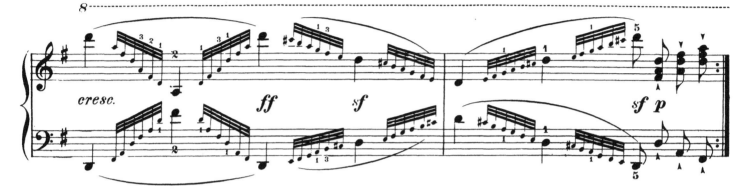

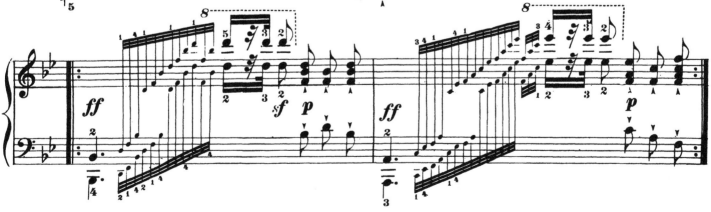

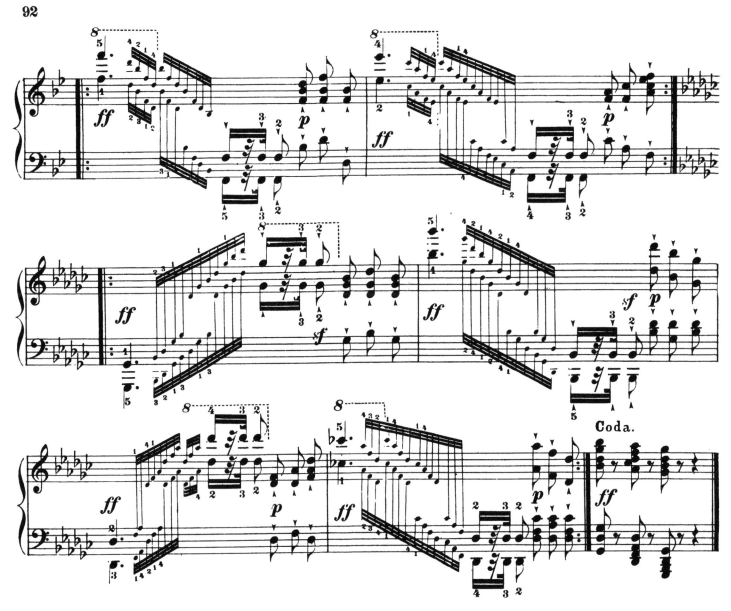

Play each repeat 16 times.

Allegro vivace. ($\stackrel{}{=}$ 72)

40.

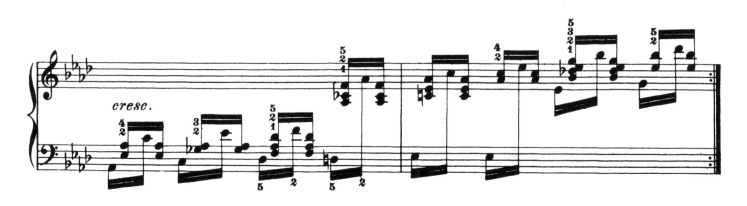

Coda.

Play each repeat 20 times.

Allegro moderato. (♩=132.)

41.

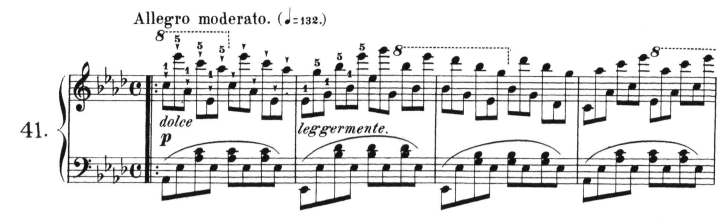

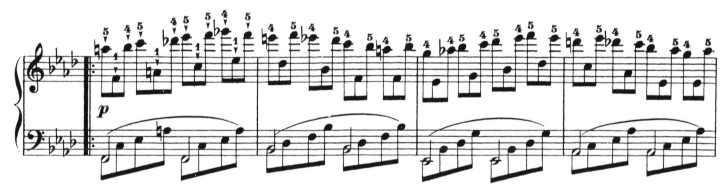

12726

Play each repeat 20 times.

42.

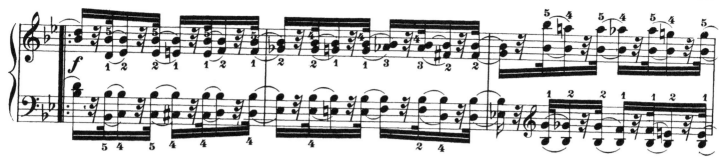

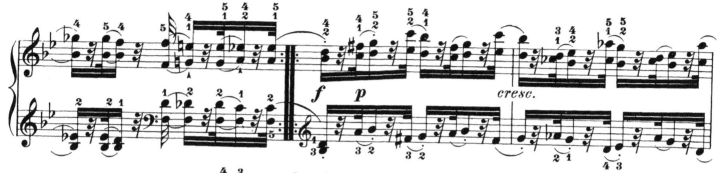

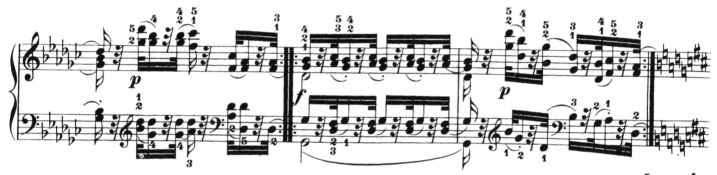

12726

Play each repeat 20 times.

Allegro non troppo. (♩=120.)

43.

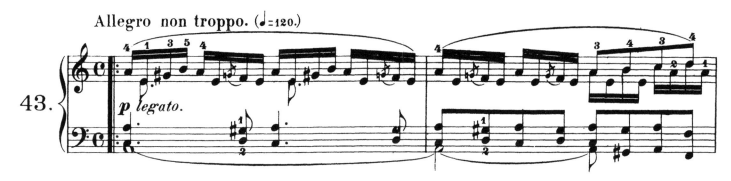

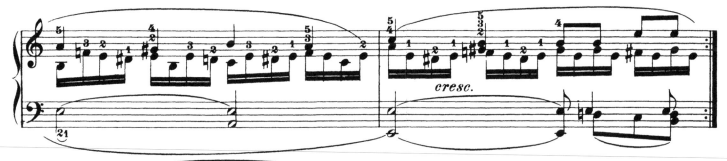

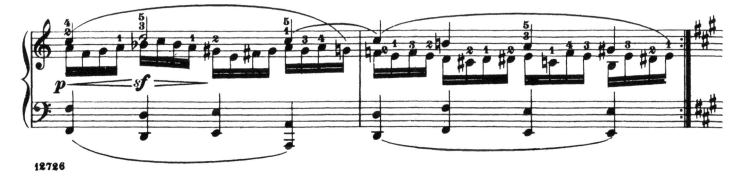

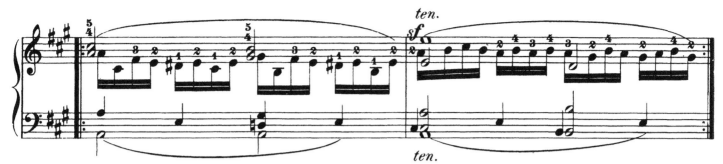

Play each repeat 12 times.

44.

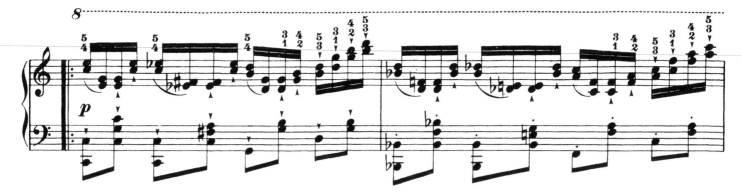

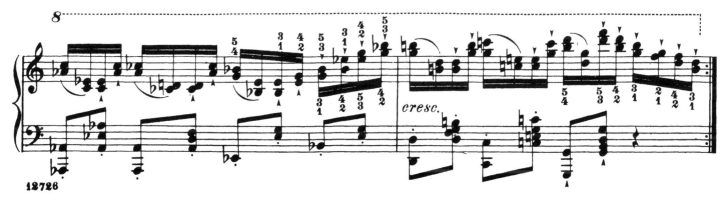

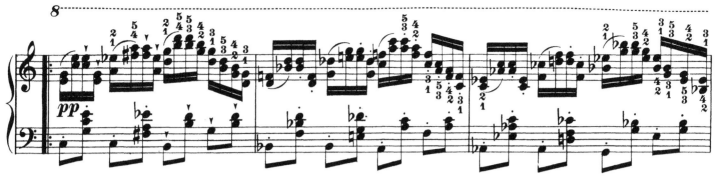

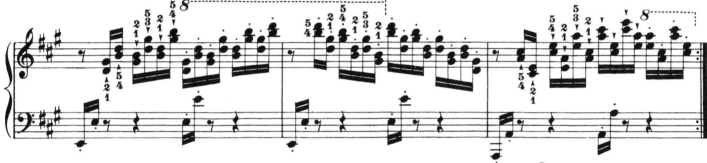

12726

School of the Virtuoso.

Play each repeat 20 times.

Allegro molto. (♩.= 76.)

C. CZERNY. Op. 365, Book IV.

45.

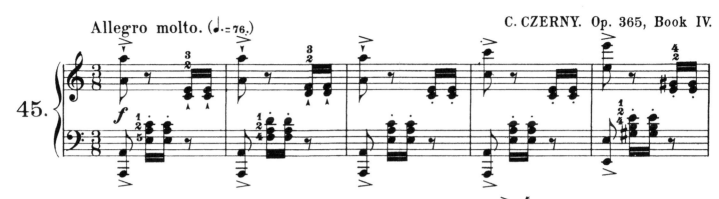

Play each repeat 12 times.

Allegro vivace. ($\bullet$=126.)

46.

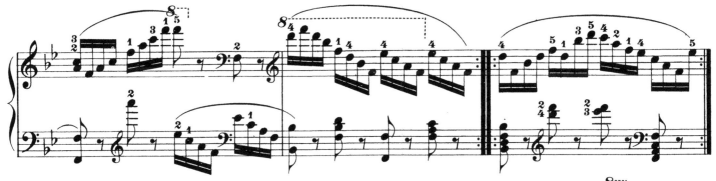

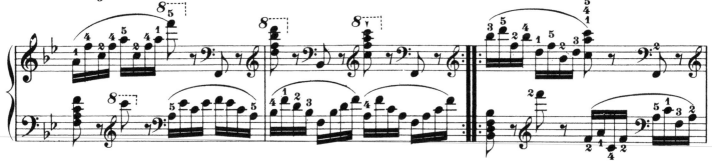

Coda.

12726

Play each repeat 24 times.

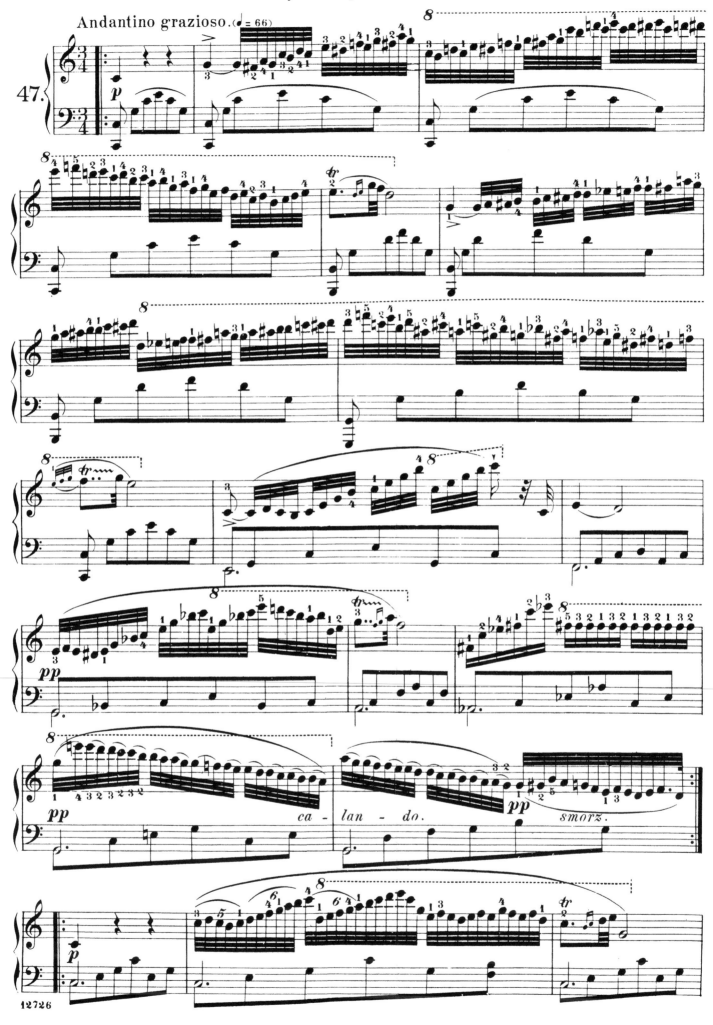

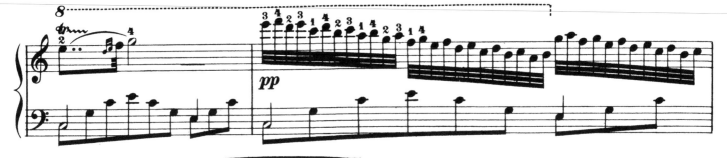

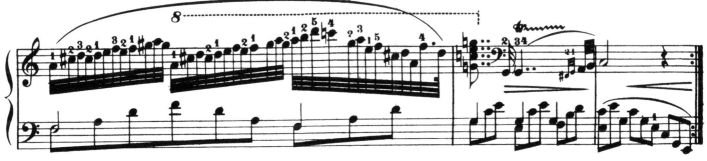

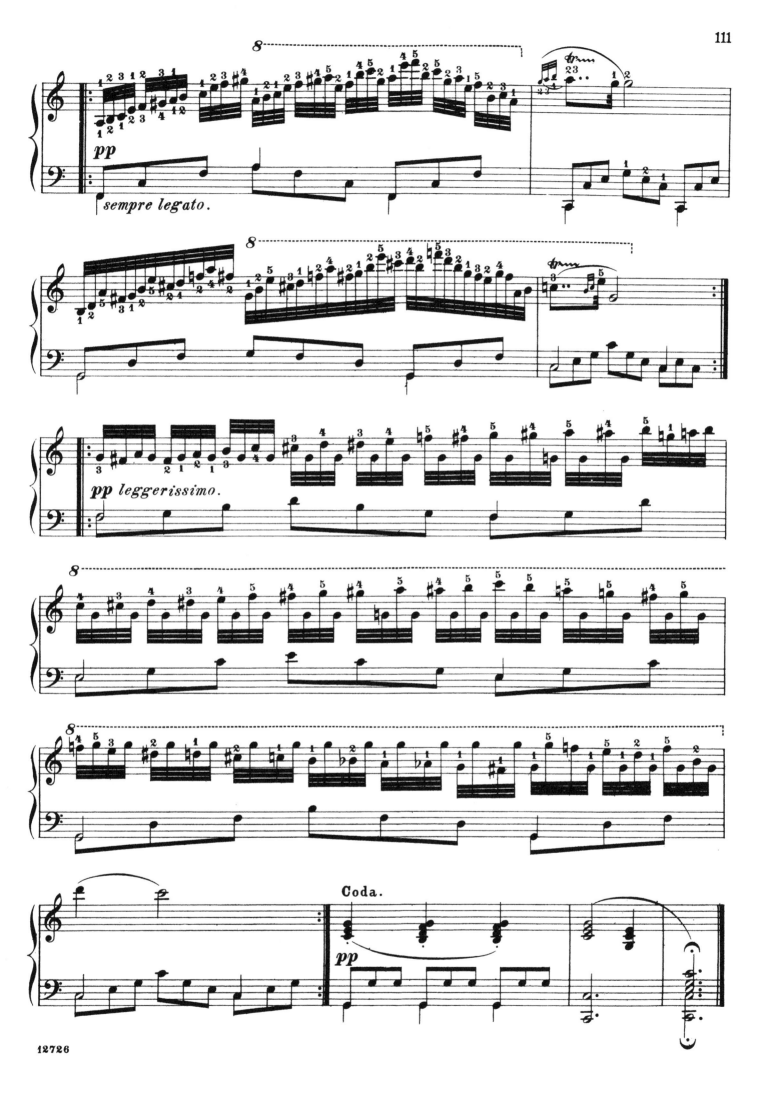

Play each repeat 30 times.

Allegro vivace. ($\downarrow$ = 104)

48.

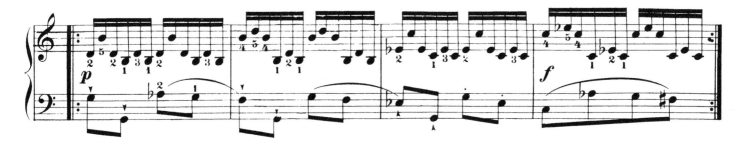

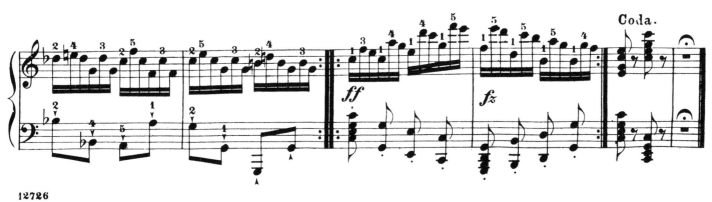

Allegro non troppo. (♩= 112) Play each repeat 30 times.

49.

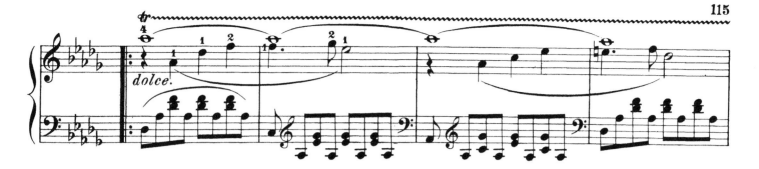

Play each repeat 20 times.

50.

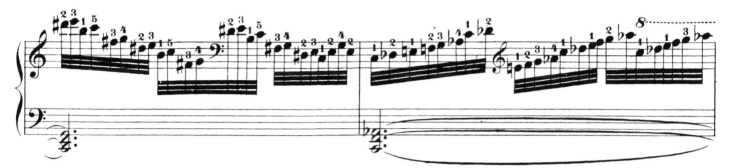

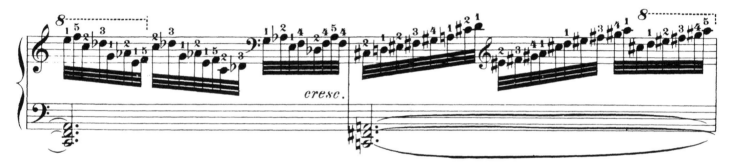

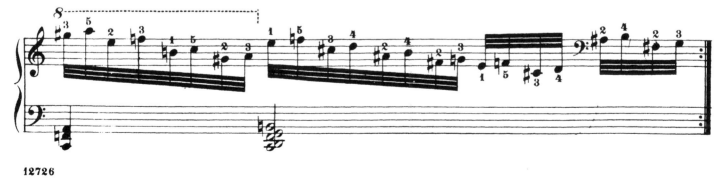

Play each repeat 20 times.

51.

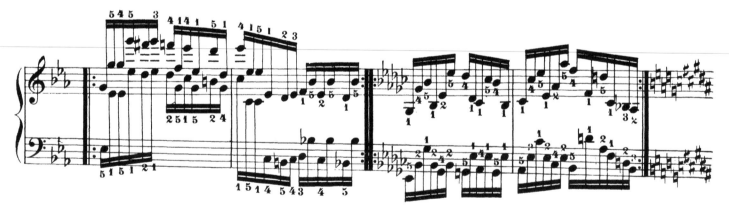

molto leggiero.

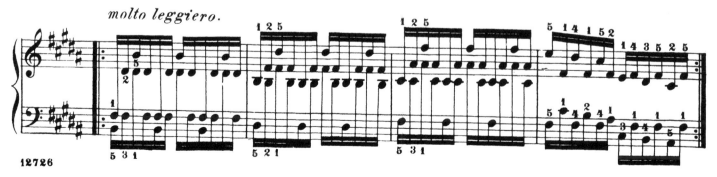

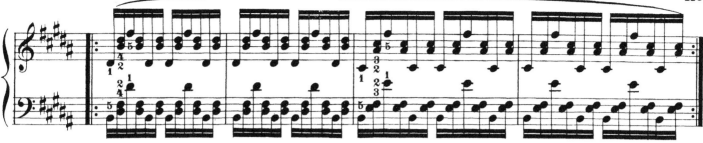

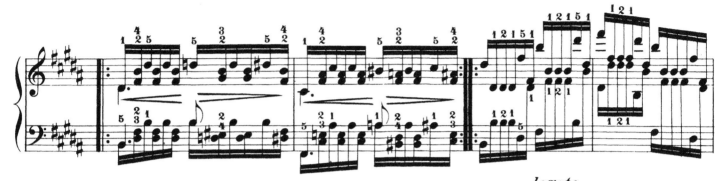

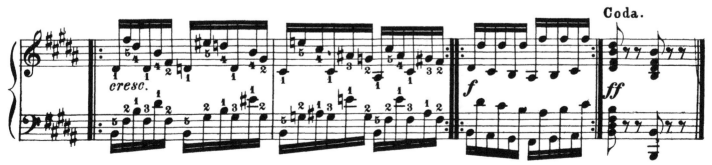

Play each repeat 16 times.

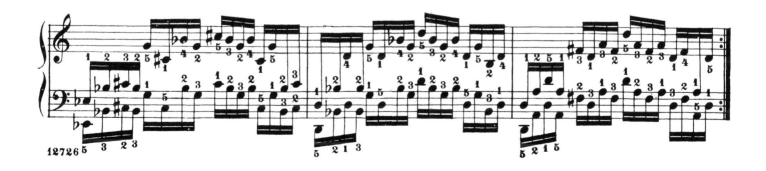

12726

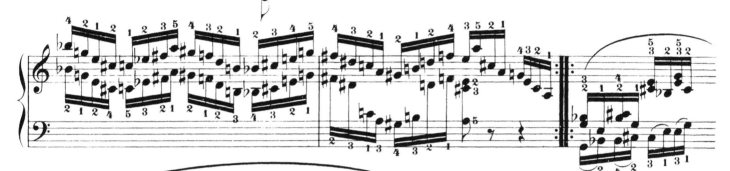

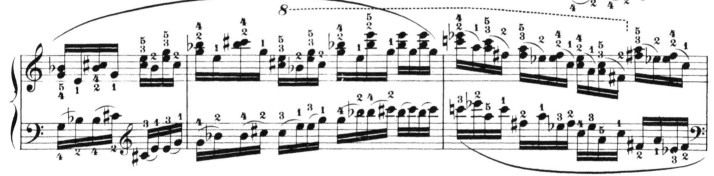

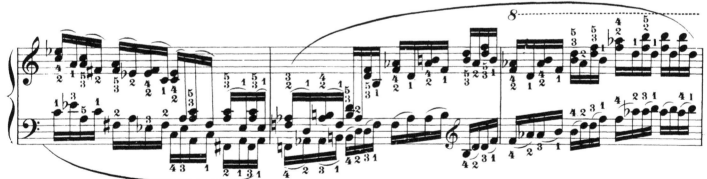

Coda.

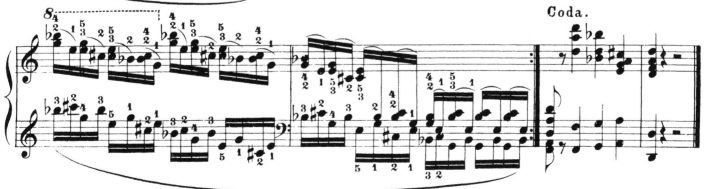

Play each repeat 12 times.

Allegro vivace. (♩ = 120)

53.

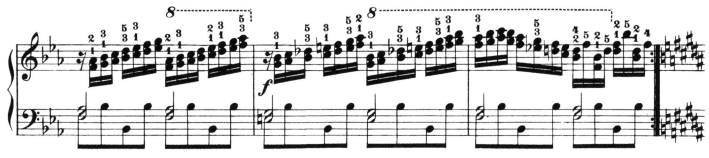

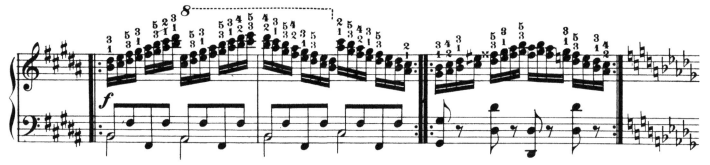

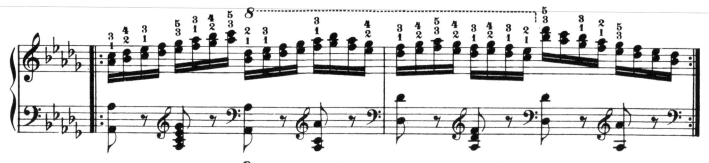

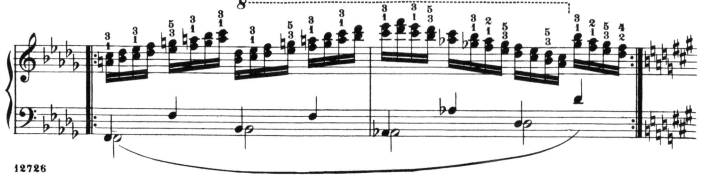

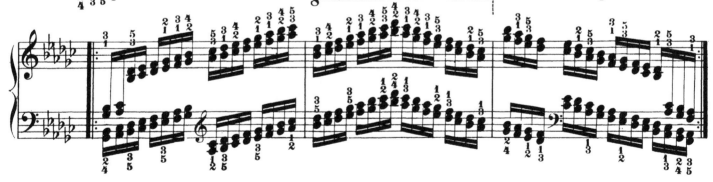

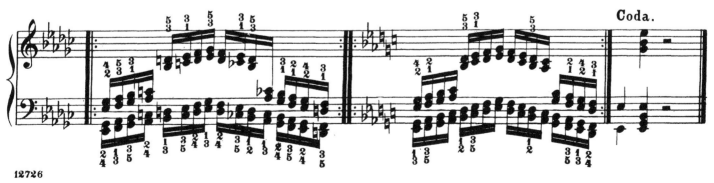

Play each repeat 16 times.

54.

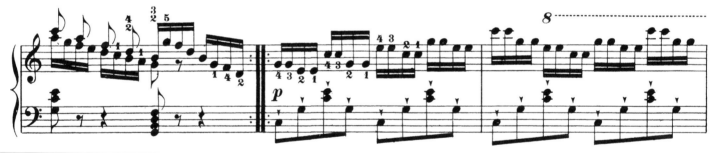

Play each repeat 16 times.

55.

Coda.

Play each repeat 30 times.

Molto Allegro. (♩=126)

56.

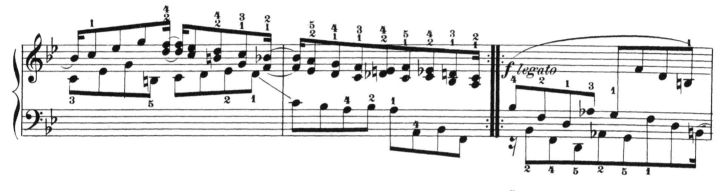

Play each repeat 20 times.

Play each repeat 16 times.

58.

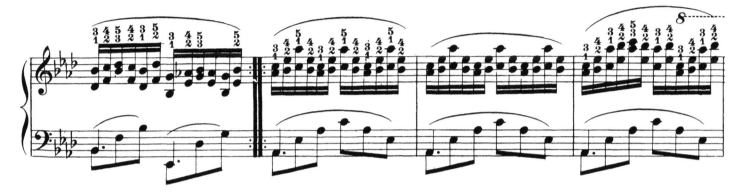

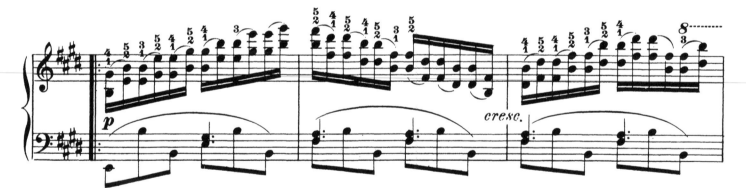

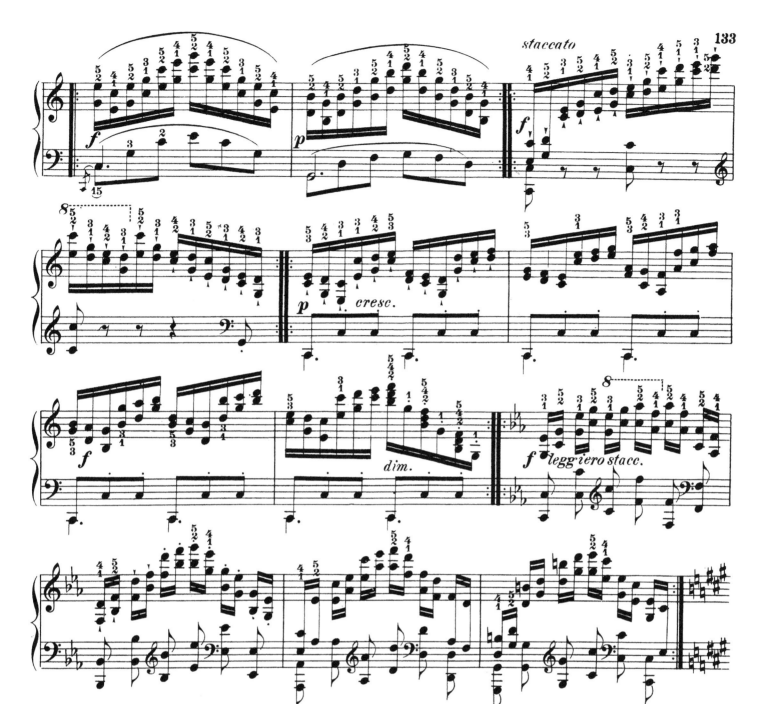

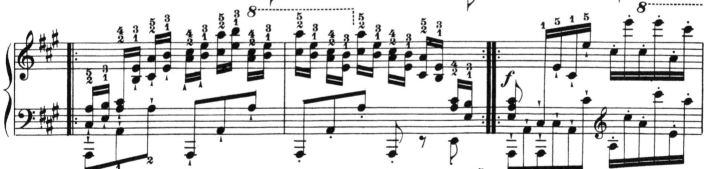

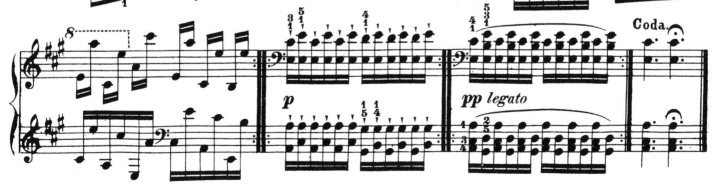

Play each repeat 30 times.

59.

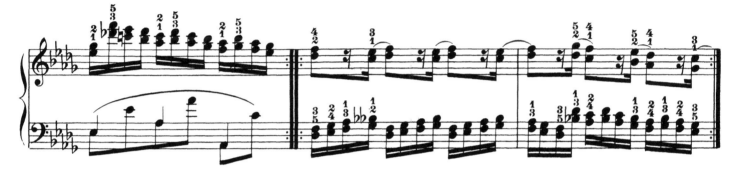

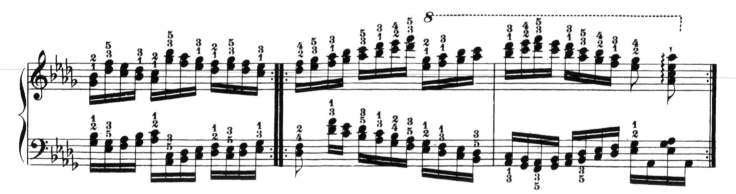

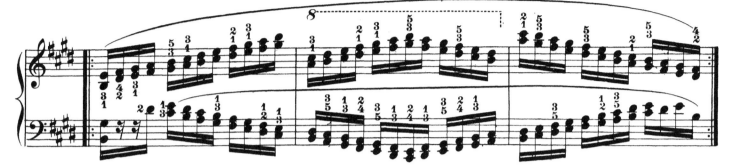

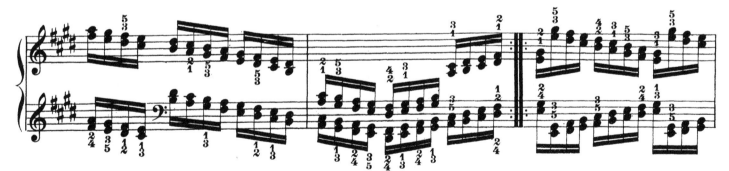

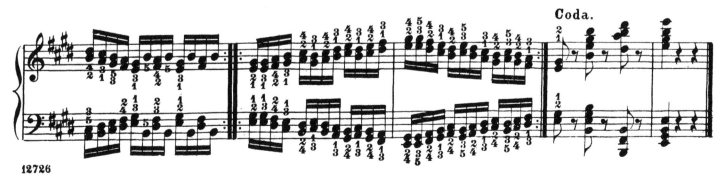

Play each repeat 16 times.

60.

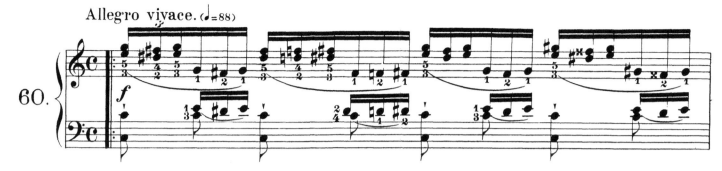

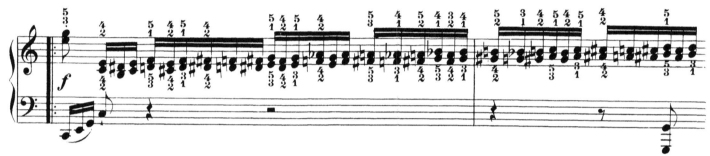

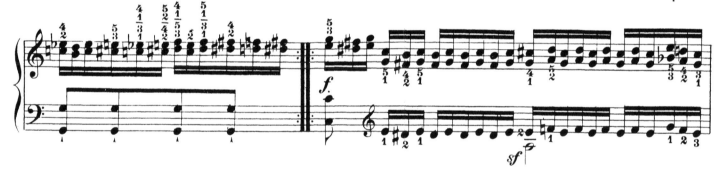

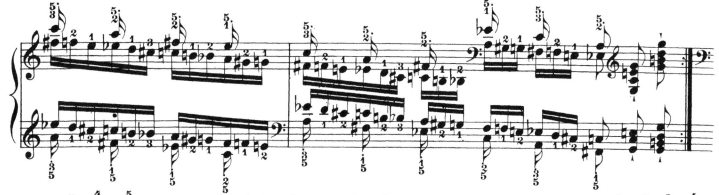

12726